Three Rings Tarot

Three Rings
To Guide Them All

Composed & Written by:
Worden Franklin Morrison

Three Rings Tarot
Three Rings
To Guide Them All
Composed & Written by:
Worden Franklin Morrison

The content of this book has been
completely theorized and developed by
Worden Franklin Morrison.

The writings and illustrations contained within this book are provided to you, from me, with the hope that your life will be greatly enhanced by them. I have theorized and developed the knowledge within this book through deep thought of my own, through reflections upon books and movies of my past, and through my own past experiences with the people and surroundings of my life. I have kept this book purposely short at 40 pages in honor of the King of the Earth, the King of the Water, the King of the Plants, and the King of the Sky.

Three Rings Tarot

Long ago, before the time of man, the twelve Areans of the three thousand galaxies decided that each galaxy should have a great process that spoke life calculations to the rest of the areas of that galaxy. The twelve Areans decided that a device in the center of a galaxy should be placed and be called an arial, devices in the galactic areas of a galaxy should be placed and be called spirals, devices in the galactic systems of a galaxy should be placed and be called pyramils, and devices in the galactic solars of a galaxy should be placed and be called stars. The twelve Areans then decided that every particle that would exist within a galaxy should be of a type that would commune with the life calculations through a process to be known as the raybeam. The twelve Areans then decided that the overall device that was to be comprised of an arial, the spirals, the pyramils, and the stars would be known as the arch, the process of the arch speaking the life calculations would be known as amendean, and the life calculations spoken by amendean would be known as the beacon. The twelve Areans in kindness also added lighthouses and spirits to the arch in order for people to be able to influence life calculations in their galaxy by using a carding system known as tarot.

Compass Rose Examples

The following images, made with compass roses, partially show you a device that I believe to be in large spheres and all of the stars throughout our galaxy. I believe that these devices are used to communicate life calculations to all living things within our galaxy. I also believe that these devices comprise a huge network throughout our galaxy, which I have termed 'Arch'.

Before a galaxy is ever used, all objects within the galaxy, including the arch, must be put into predefined positions. All objects within a galaxy remain still, constant, and dormant until life is introduced into that galaxy.

An eye of the device in an inactive state before it is ever used and before any life is placed within a galaxy.

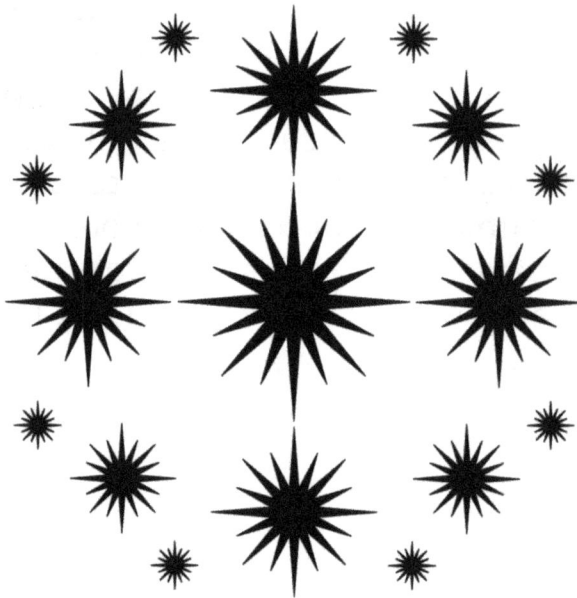

Once life is introduced into a galaxy, the objects within the galaxy move, become variable, and have life. The arch becomes active, and all of the arch's chambers move into a read state, which enables the arch to receive life calculation transmissions from all parts of the galaxy. These life calculations are read, accepted or rejected, and then all of the accepted life calculations for all destinations within the galaxy are formed into one of four large galactic transmission files for later transmission to all parts of the galaxy.

An eye of the device in an active read state after life has been introduced into a galaxy.

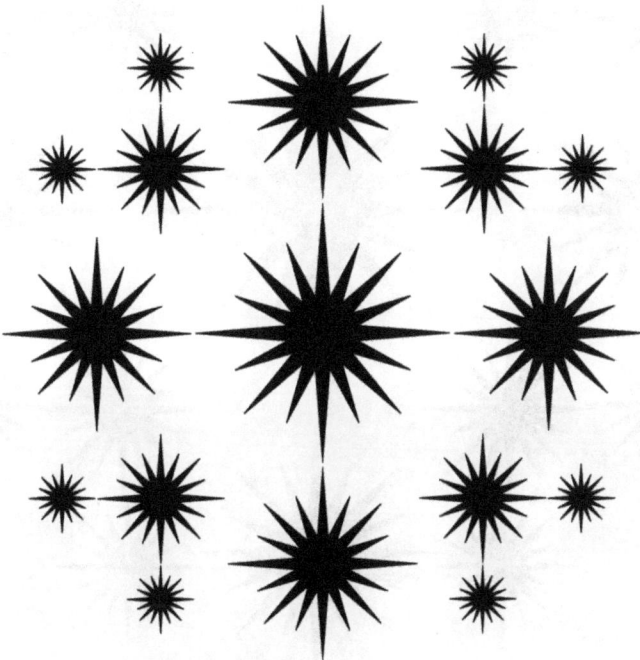

Once the life calculations have been accepted and have been formed into files, the eye prepares to send its file throughout the galaxy. In the first stage of sending the file, the chambers of the eye expand into their send file position.

An eye of the device in the first stage of its life calculations transmission.

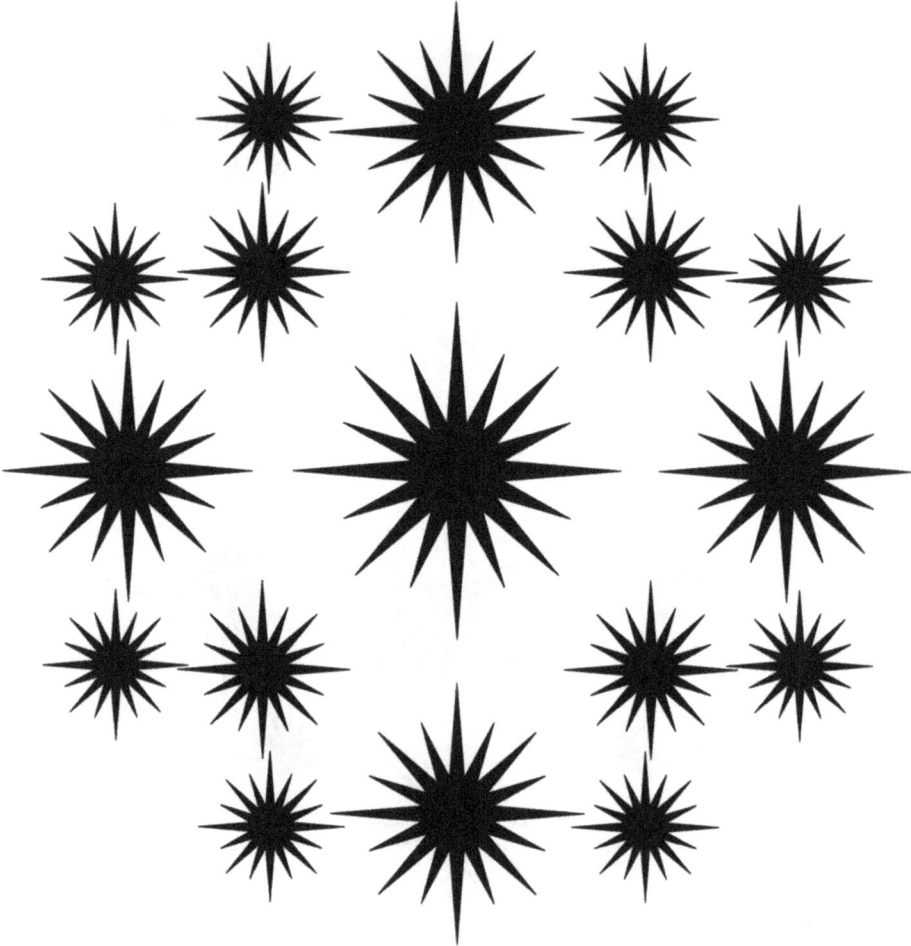

In the second stage of sending the file, the rooms of the center chamber align with their center house, making the center chamber active.

An eye of the device in the second stage
of its life calculations transmission.

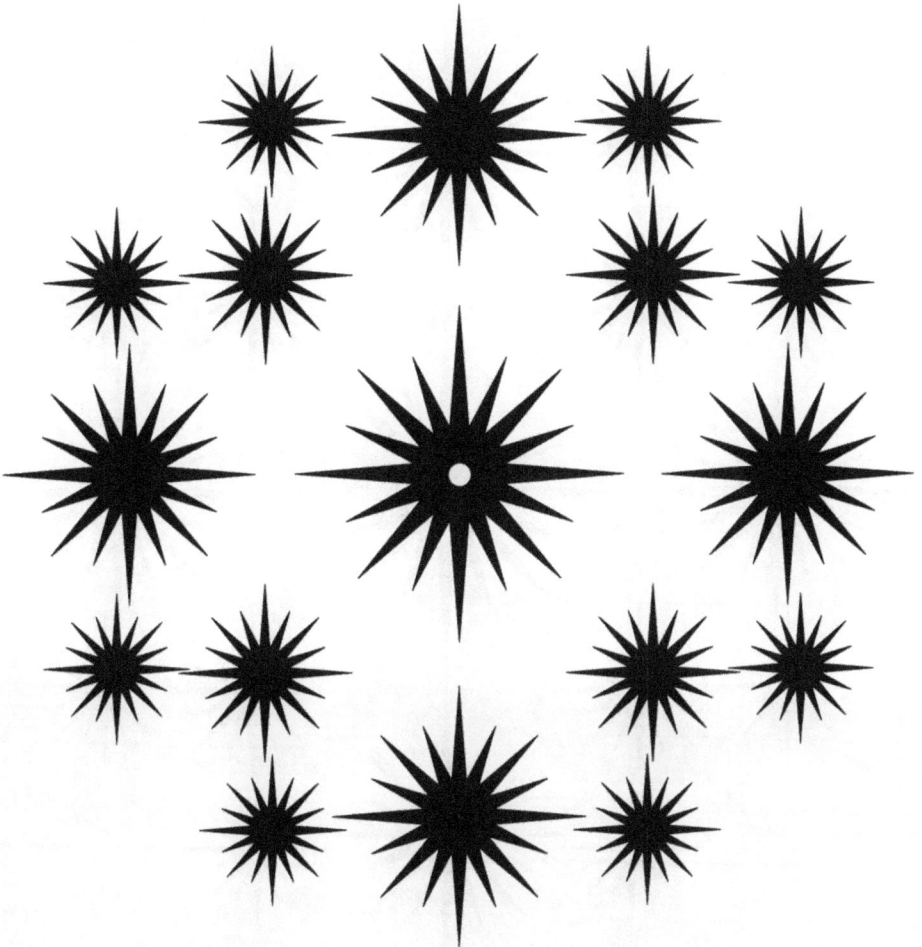

In the third stage of sending the file, the rooms of the second chambers align with their center houses, then the second chambers align with the first chamber, making the second chambers active. The first ring has now been formed.

An eye of the device in the third stage
of its life calculations transmission.

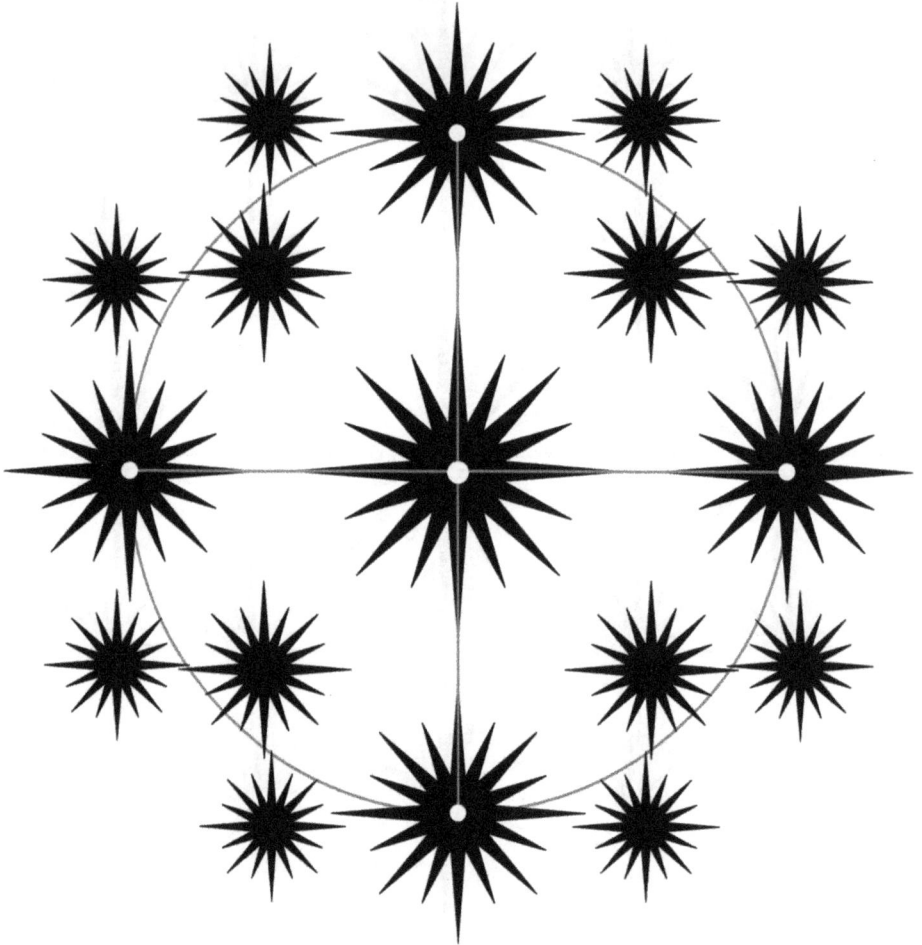

In the fourth stage of sending the file, the rooms of the third chambers align with their center houses, then the third chambers align with the first chamber, making the third chambers active. The second ring has now been formed.

An eye of the device in the fourth stage
of its life calculations transmission.

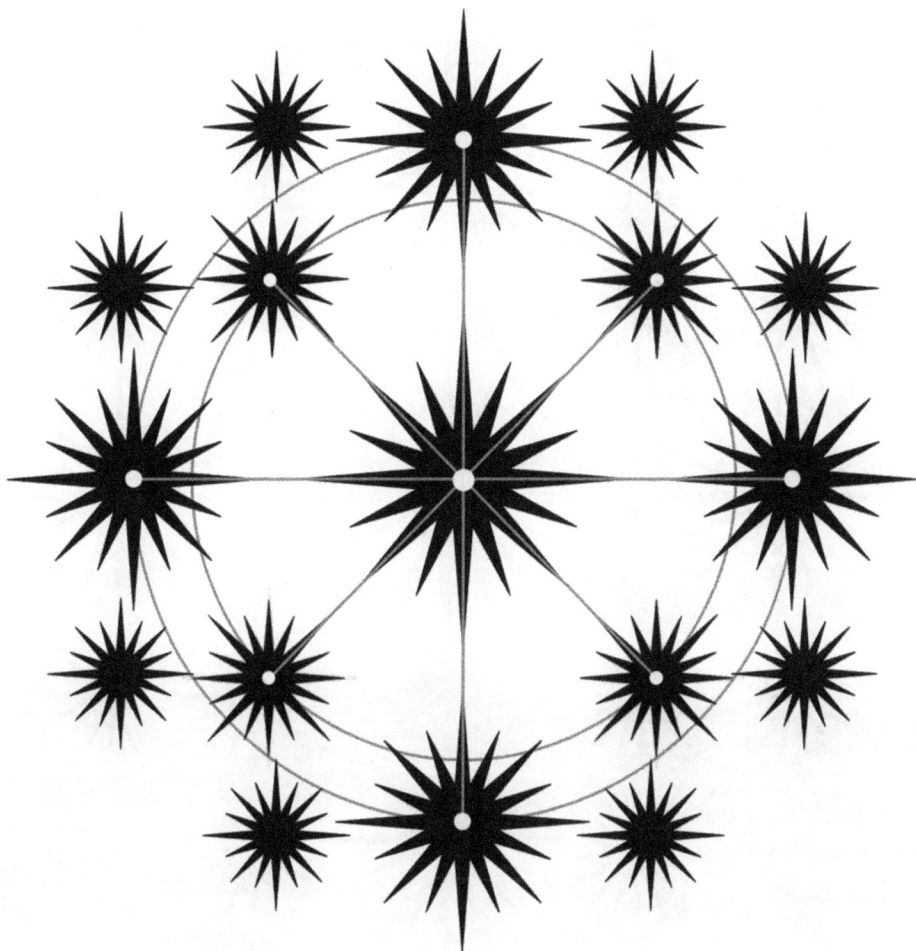

In the fifth stage of sending the file, the rooms of the fourth chambers align with their center houses, then the fourth chambers align with the first chamber, making the fourth chambers active. The third ring has now been formed, and the file is sent to all parts of the galaxy.

An eye of the device in the fifth stage
of its life calculations transmission.

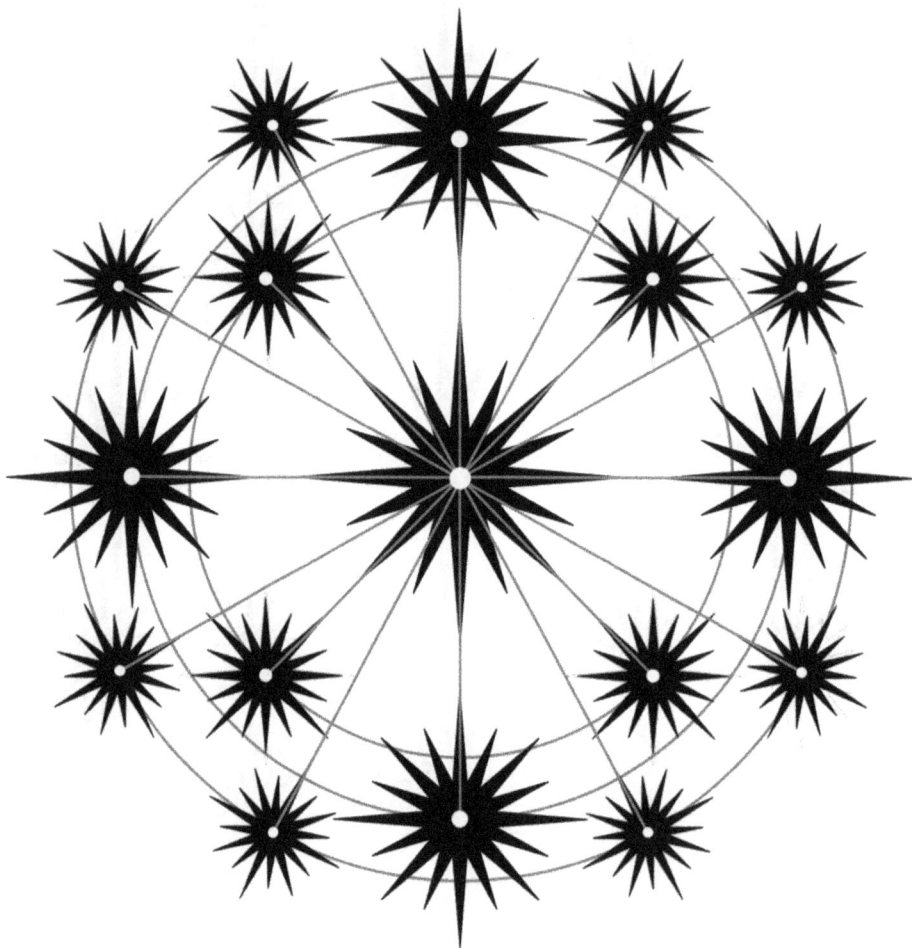

The Arch in Greater Detail

The following descriptions outline the arch and its associated components in much greater detail than in the previous compass rose examples. The illustrations that follow the descriptions are made with the two most basic of shapes, which are squares and circles, and the illustrations should give you a good visual understanding of the arch. Understanding the process of the arch gathering life calculations and sending life calculations throughout your galaxy will give you a greater appreciation of your galaxy's arch.

An arial consists of a core with four towers attached to the core, and one eye attached to each tower. Onto each eye is one crown's chamber with four kings' chambers attached to the crown's chamber, one queen's chamber attached to each king's chamber, and two assistants' chambers attached to each queen's chamber. A spiral consists of a core with four towers attached to the core, and one eye attached to each tower. Onto each eye is one crown's chamber with four kings' chambers attached to the crown's chamber, one queen's chamber attached to each king's chamber, and two assistants' chambers attached to each queen's chamber. A pyramil consists of a core with eight towers attached to the core, and one eye attached to each tower. Onto each eye is one crown's chamber with four kings' chambers attached to the crown's chamber, one queen's chamber attached to each king's chamber, and two assistants' chambers attached to each queen's chamber. A star consists of a core with one, two, or three towers attached to the core, and one eye attached to each tower. Onto each eye is one crown's chamber with four kings' chambers attached to the crown's chamber, one queen's chamber attached to each king's chamber, and two assistants' chambers attached to each queen's chamber. The kings' chambers form the first ring, the queens' chambers form the second ring, and the assistants' chambers form the third ring.

Each chamber is nearly the same in design, except that the chambers' sizes incrementally decrease from the crown's chamber to the assistants' chambers. A chamber consists of a center house with four first rooms attached to the center house, one second room attached to each first room, and two third rooms attached to each second room. Each chamber communicates with the other chambers of its eye with a lightcrown at the center of each chamber's center house, and each room of each chamber communicates with its lightcrown with a lighthouse at the center of each room.

Before any galaxy is ever used, the arial, spirals, pyramils, stars, and raybeam are in their rest states, and they stay in their rest states until they are needed for galactic life transmissions. **refer to illustration 1**

Once a galaxy becomes inhabited, the arial, spirals, pyramils, and stars are moved into their read states, the raybeam is activated, and the arch is ready to read life calculations for later transmission. Every single day within a galaxy, life calculations are sent into the arch for examination, life calculations are examined to be used within the beacon, and the beacon is sent throughout a galaxy with amendean. **refer to illustration 2**

Once the beacon is ready to be sent, amendean is activated. The arial moves into its send sut state and transmits send sut to the spirals, which move into their send sut states and transmit send sut to the pyramils, which move into their send sut states and transmit send sut to the stars, which move into their send sut states. Then the stars transmit send sot back to the pyramils, which transmit send sot back to the spirals, which transmit send sot back to the arial. In the send sut state for each eye in the arch, the crown's chamber, the kings' chambers, the queens' chambers, and the assistants' chambers placements expand, as do the rooms for each of the chambers. **refer to illustration 3**

Then the arial moves into its send sot state and transmits send sot to the spirals, which move into their send sot states and transmit send sot to the pyramils, which move into their send sot states and transmit send sot to the stars, which move into their send sot states. Then the stars transmit send sit back to the pyramils, which transmit send sit back to the spirals, which transmit send sit back to the arial. The alignment of amendean has begun. In the send sot state for each eye in the arch, the crown's chamber's rooms rotate to align properly with the crown's chamber's center house. **refer to illustration 4**

Then the arial moves into its send sit state and transmits send sit to the spirals, which move into their send sit states and transmit send sit to the pyramils, which move into their send sit states and transmit send sit to the stars, which move into their send sit states. Then the stars transmit send set back to the pyramils, which transmit send set back to the spirals, which transmit send set back to the arial, and the first ring is formed. In the send sit state for each eye in the arch, each king's chamber's rooms rotate to align properly with their king's chamber's center house, and the kings' chambers rotate to align properly with the crown's chamber's center house. **refer to illustration 5**

Then the arial moves into its send set state and transmits send set to the spirals, which move into their send set states and transmit send set to the pyramils, which move into their send set states and transmit send set to the stars, which move into their send set states. Then the stars transmit send sat back to the pyramils, which transmit send sat back to the spirals, which transmit send sat back to the arial, and the second ring is formed. In the send set state for each eye in the arch, each queen's chamber's rooms rotate to align properly with their queen's chamber's center house, and the queens' chambers rotate to align properly with the crown's chamber's center house. **refer to illustration 6**

Then the arial moves into its send sat state and transmits send sat to the spirals, which move into their send sat states and transmit send sat to the pyramils, which move into their send sat states and transmit send sat to the stars, which move into their send sat states and transmit send sat to the raybeam. The third ring is formed, and amendean is now completely aligned. In the send sat state for each eye in the arch, each assistant's chamber's rooms rotate to align properly with their assistant's chamber's center house, and the assistants' chambers rotate to align properly with the crown's chamber's center house. **refer to illustration 7**

Then the arial lights the beacon and transmits the beacon to the spirals, which transmit the beacon to the pyramils, which transmit the beacon to the stars, which transmit the beacon to the raybeam, which communes with all particles and all living things within its area.

Once the beacon has been completely sent, the raybeam transmits sent sat to the stars, which move into their sent sat states and transmit sent sat to the pyramils, which move into their sent sat states and transmit sent sat to the spirals, which move into their sent sat states and transmit sent sat to the arial, which moves into its sent sat state. Then the arial transmits sent set back to the spirals, which transmit sent set back to the pyramils, which transmit sent set back to the stars. The third ring is unformed, and the dealignment of amendean has begun. In the sent sat state for each eye in the arch, the assistants' chambers rotate to dealign from the crown's chamber's center house, and each assistant's chamber's rooms rotate to dealign from their assistant's chamber's center house. **refer to illustration 8**

Then the stars move into their sent set states and transmit sent set to the pyramils, which move into their sent set states and transmit sent set to the spirals, which move into their sent set states and transmit sent set to the arial, which moves into its sent set state. Then the arial transmits sent sit back to the spirals, which transmit sent sit back to the pyramils, which transmit sent sit back to the stars, and the second ring is unformed. In the sent set state for each eye in the arch, the queens' chambers rotate to dealign from the crown's chamber's center house, and each queen's chamber's rooms rotate to dealign from their queen's chamber's center house. **refer to illustration 9**

Then the stars move into their sent sit states and transmit sent sit to the pyramils, which move into their sent sit states and transmit sent sit to the spirals, which move into their sent sit states and transmit sent sit to the arial, which moves into its sent sit state. Then the arial transmits sent sot back to the spirals, which transmit sent sot back to the pyramils, which transmit sent sot back to the stars, and the first ring is unformed. In the sent sit state for each eye in the arch, the kings' chambers rotate to dealign from the crown's chamber's center house, and each king's chamber's rooms rotate to dealign from their king's chamber's center house. **refer to illustration 10**

Then the stars move into their sent sot states and transmit sent sot to the pyramils, which move into their sent sot states and transmit sent sot to the spirals, which move into their sent sot states and transmit sent sot to the arial, which moves into its sent sot state. Then the arial transmits sent sut back to the spirals, which transmit sent sut back to the pyramils, which transmit sent sut back to the stars, and amendean is completely dealigned. In the sent sot state for each eye in the arch, the crown's chamber's rooms rotate to dealign with the crown's chamber's center house. **refer to illustration 11**

Then the stars move into their sent sut states and transmit sent sut to the pyramils, which move into their sent sut states and transmit sent sut to the spirals, which move into their sent sut states and transmit sent sut to the arial, which moves into its sent sut state. Then the arial transmits ready read back to the spirals, which transmit ready read back to the pyramils, which transmit ready read back to the stars, and amendean is now completely deactivated. The arch is in its ready read state once again, and amendean is not activated again until another beacon transmission is scheduled. In the sent sut state for each eye in the arch the crown's chamber, the kings' chambers, the queens' chambers, and the assistants' chambers placements contract as do the rooms for each of the chambers. **refer to illustration 12**

Illustration 1

Rest

Before the eye is ever used, the chambers are in their locked positions, and the rooms for each chamber are also in their locked positions. The locked positions disallow any communications to the chambers and rooms.

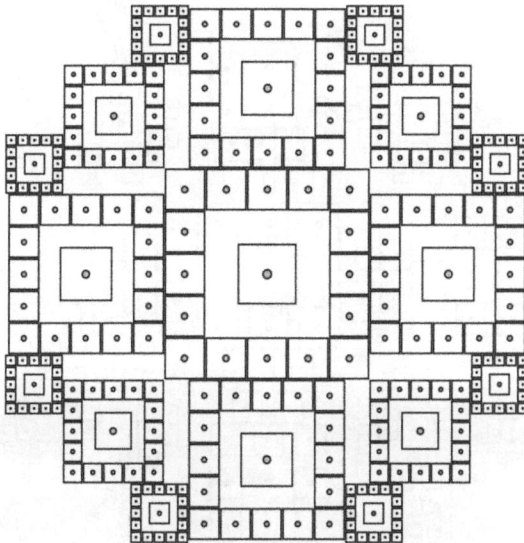

Illustration 2

Ready

Once the eye has been activated, the chambers move into their unlocked positions, and the rooms for each chamber also move into their unlocked positions. The unlocked positions allow communications to the chambers and rooms.

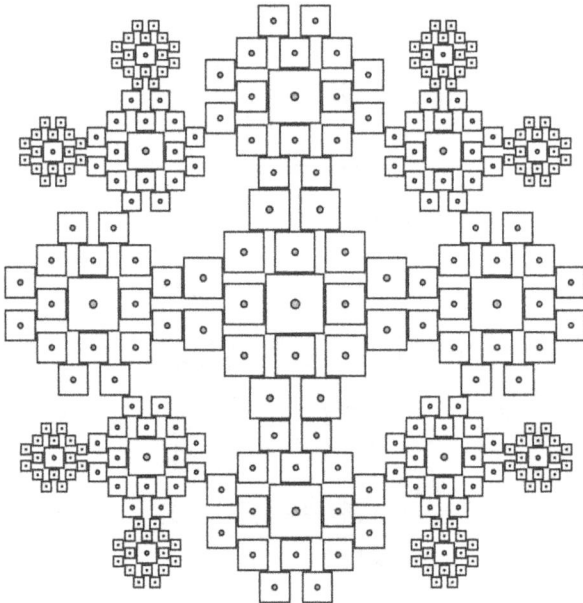

Illustration 3

Send Sut

Once life calculations have been read, recognized, and readied, the beacon is formed, and power is applied to the arch. The chambers expand, and the rooms for each chamber also expand.

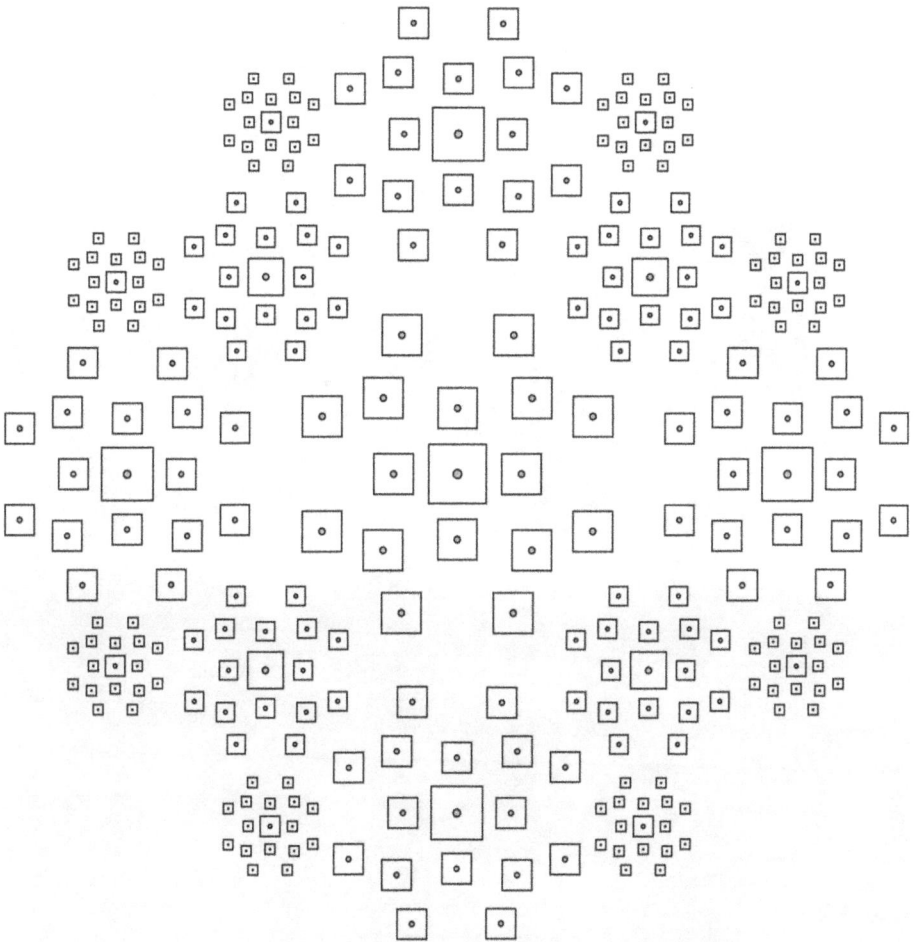

Illustration 4

Send Sot

After power has been applied to the arch, amendean begins alignment. The rooms of the crown's chamber align with the crown's chamber's center house, and the crown's chamber is now active.

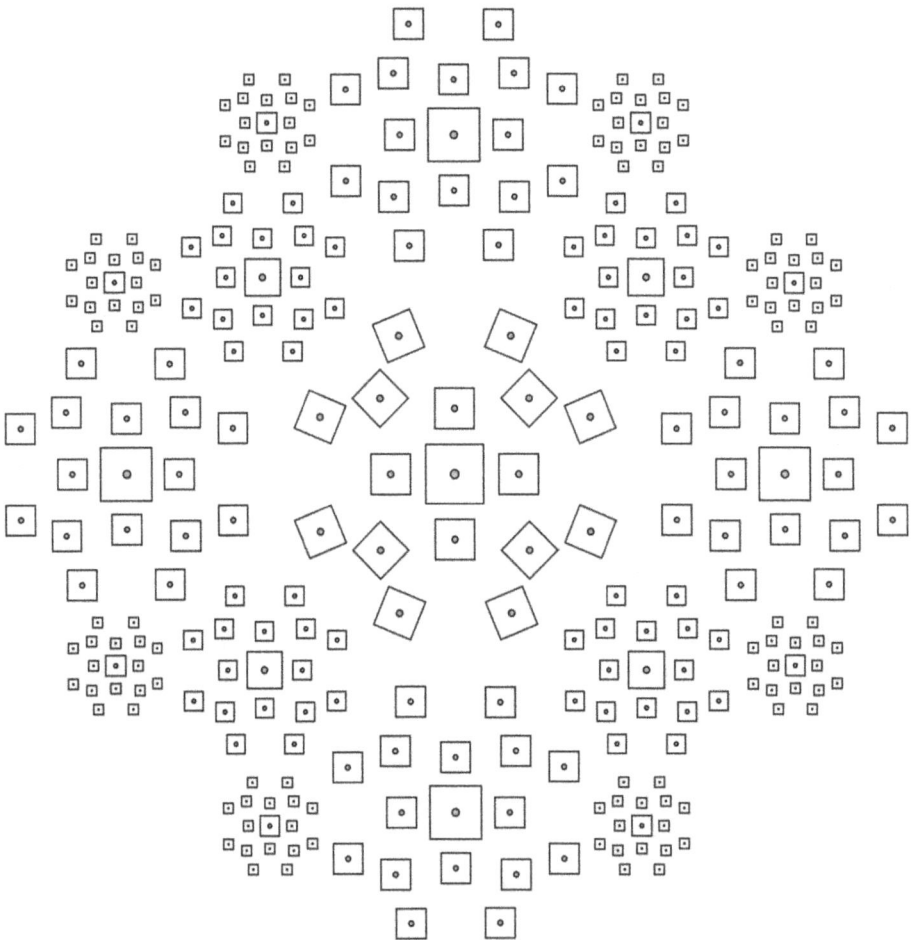

Illustration 5

Send Sit

The rooms of each king's chamber align with their king's chamber's center house, and the kings' chambers align with the crown's chamber's center house. The kings' chambers are now active, and the first ring is formed.

Illustration 6

Send Set

The rooms of each queen's chamber align with their queen's chamber's center house, and the queens' chambers align with the crown's chamber's center house. The queens' chambers are now active, and the second ring is formed.

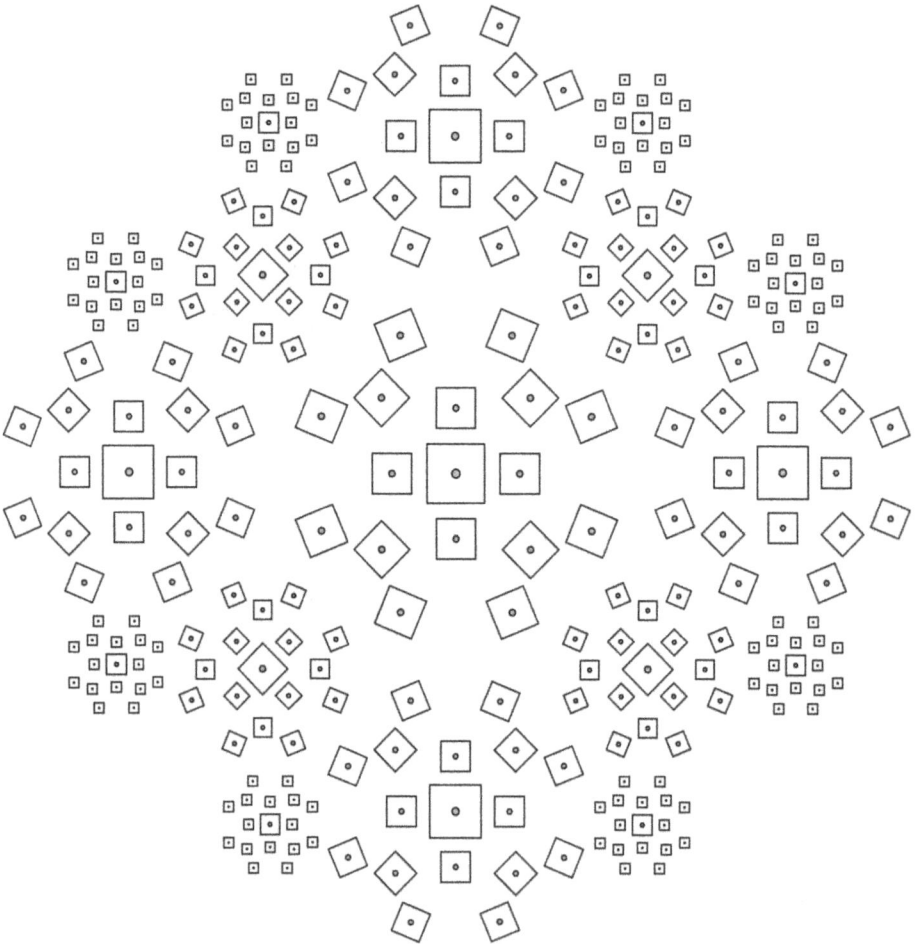

Illustration 7

Send Sat

The rooms of each assistant's chamber align with their assistant's chamber's center house, and the assistants' chambers align with the crown's chamber's center house. The assistants' chambers are now active, the third ring is formed, and the beacon is sent.

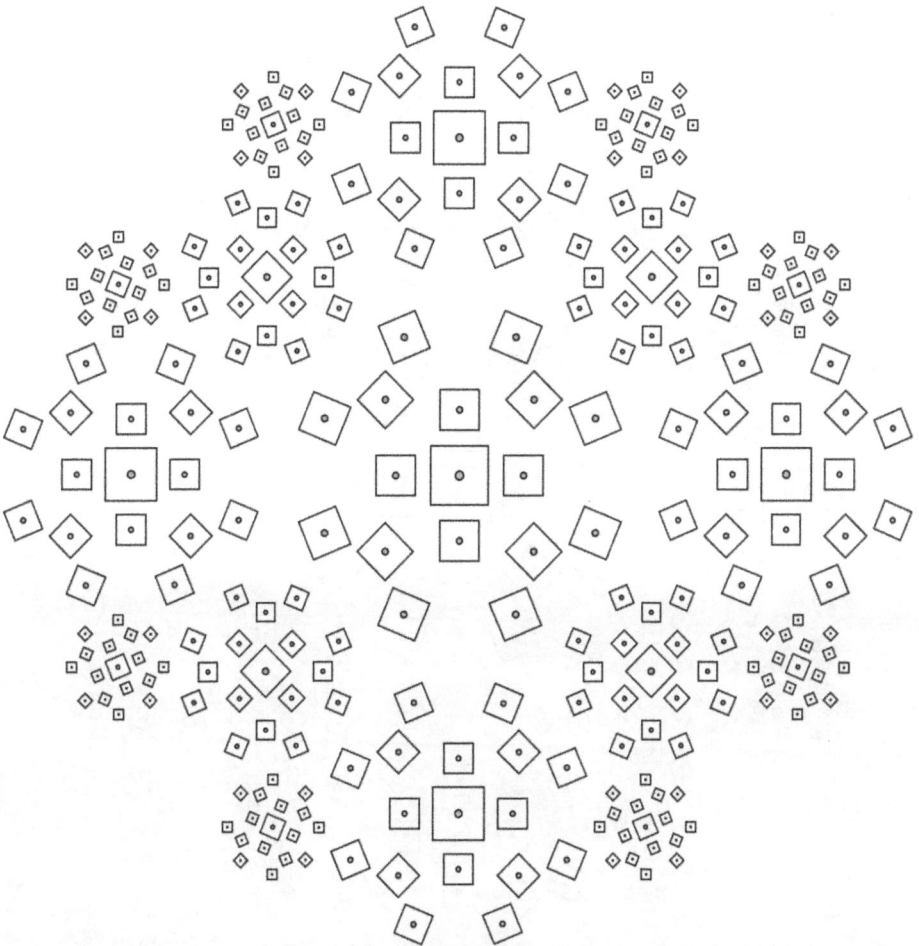

Illustration 8

Sent Sat

Once the beacon has been completely sent, the assistants' chambers dealign with the crown's chamber's center house, and the rooms of each assistant's chamber dealign with their assistant's chamber's center house. The assistants' chambers are now deactivated, the third ring is unformed, and the dealignment of amendean has begun.

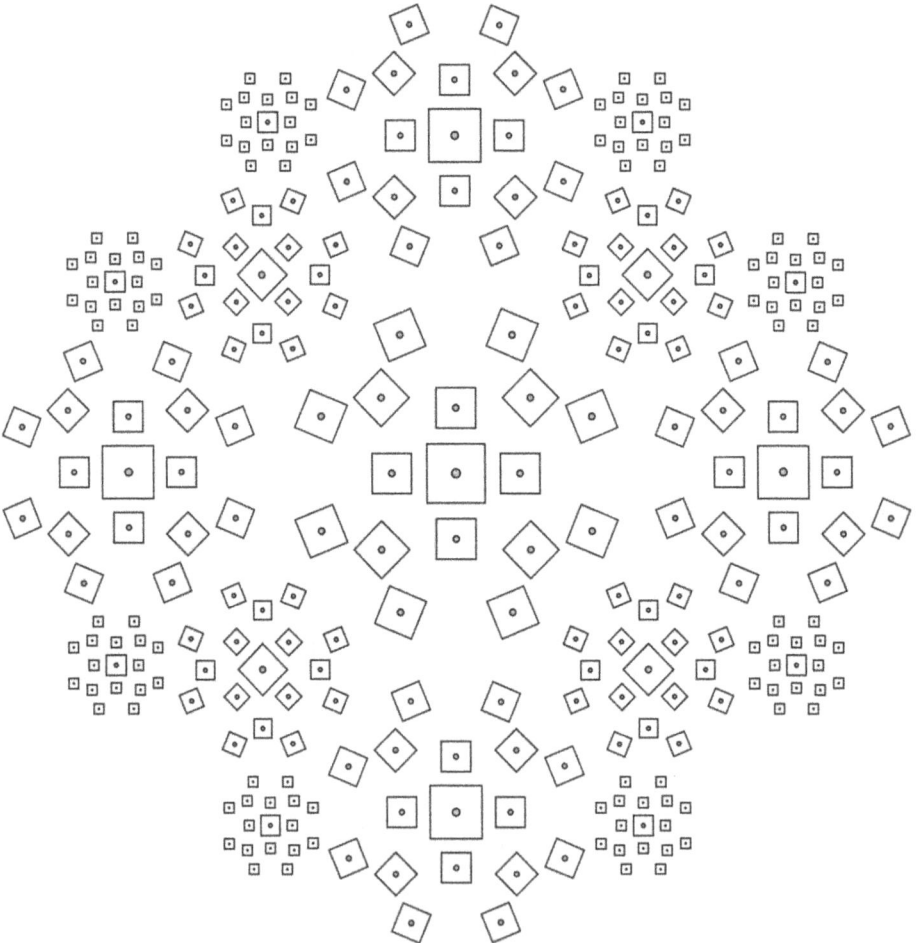

Illustration 9

Sent Set

The queens' chambers dealign with the crown's chamber's center house, and the rooms of each queen's chamber dealign with their queen's chamber's center house. The queens' chambers are now deactivated, and the second ring is unformed.

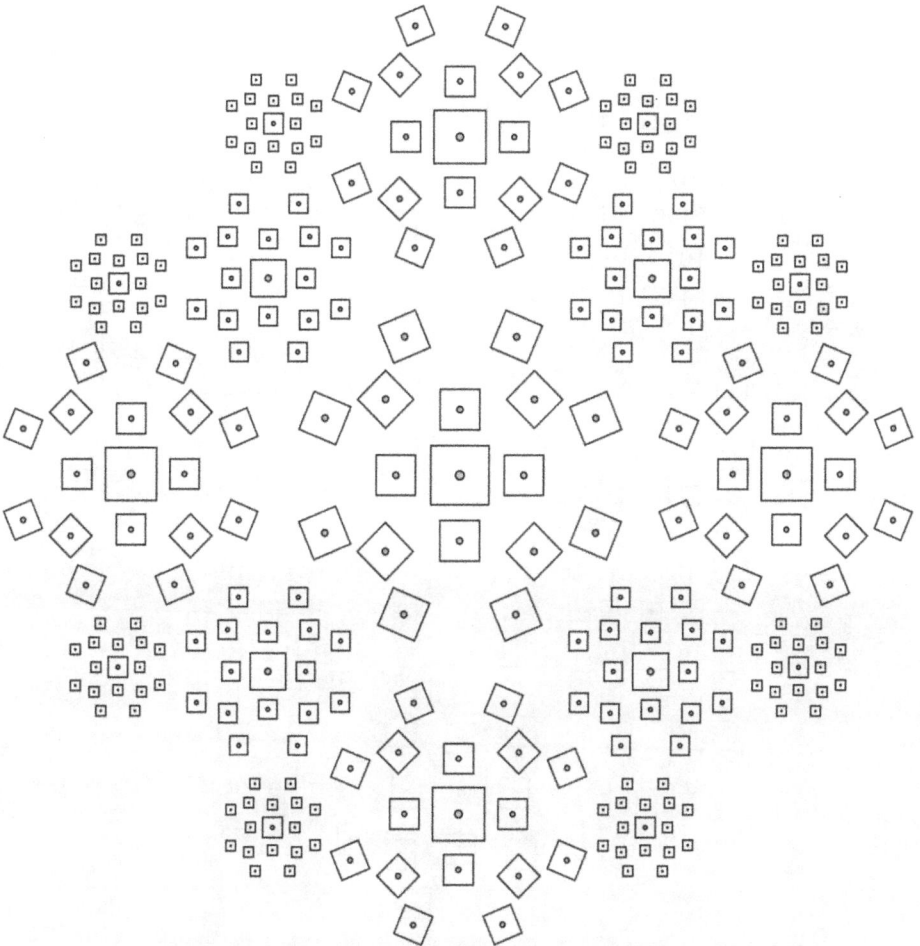

Illustration 10

Sent Sit

The kings' chambers dealign with the crown's chamber's center house, and the rooms of each king's chamber dealign with their king's chamber's center house. The kings' chambers are now deactivated, and the first ring is unformed.

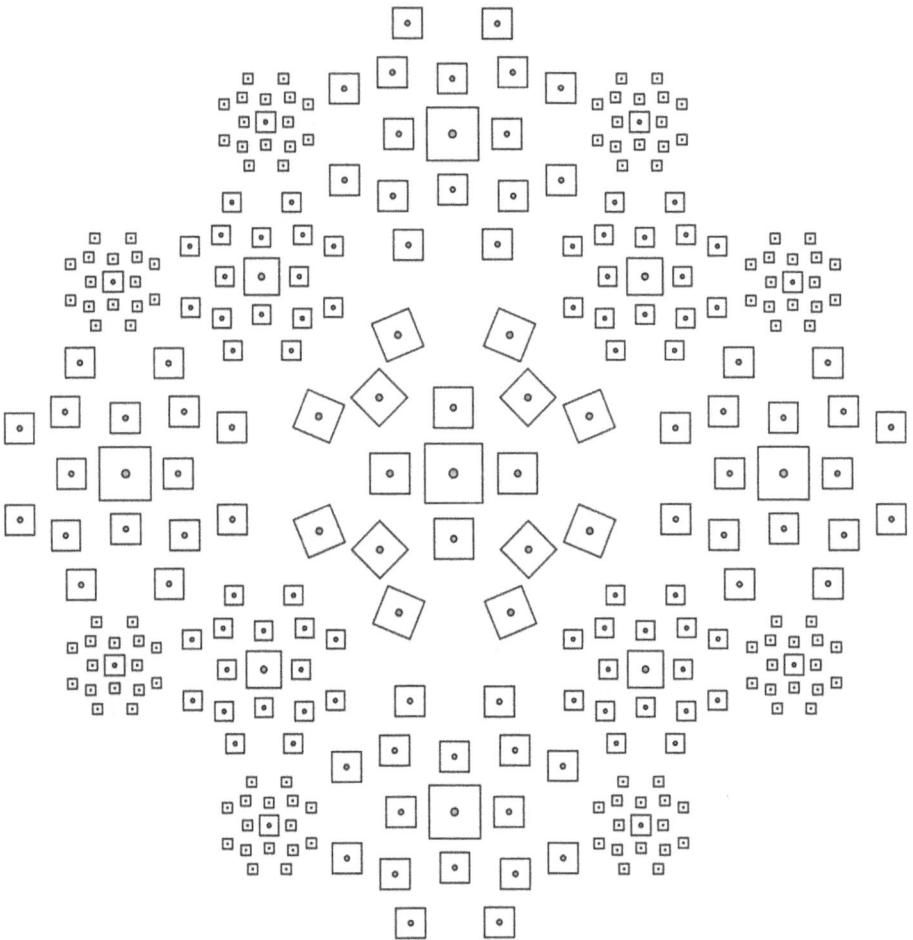

Illustration 11

Sent Sot

The rooms of the crown's chamber dealign with the crown's chamber's center house. The crown's chamber is now deactivated, and amendean is now completely dealigned.

Illustration 12

Sent Sut

The rooms for each chamber contract into their ready positions, the chambers contract into their ready read positions, and power is removed from the arch. The eye now awaits for further life calculations.

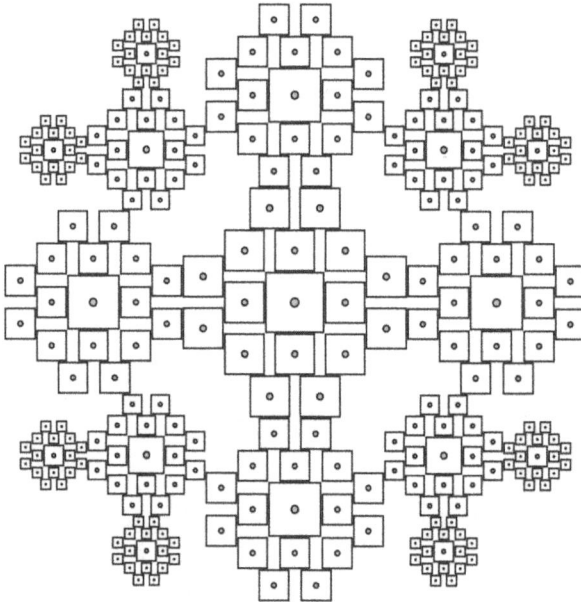

Tarot and the Arch

The following descriptions explain how to use tarot to influence life calculations within your area of your galaxy. The illustrations that follow the descriptions are made with two basic shapes, which are squares and rectangles, and the illustrations should give you a good visual understanding of how to use your tarot cards properly. Each chamber on every eye of the arch contains a lightcrown at the center with four points of entry for communion with people. In order for you to commune with the arch, you must use tarot cards arranged around a square, which forms a small beacon to your star when you place your symbol onto the square. A prior knowledge of tarot, tarot's associated images, and the spiritual relations of tarot's associated images are necessary for you to already have learned in order for you to commune life calculations with the arch in your galaxy.

A way of communicating life calculations with the arch has been provided for any person having the proper items and knowledge. Communicating life calculations with the arch can become a daily occurrence for you if you so choose. If you do choose to communicate life calculations with the arch, please read the following definitions, information, and instructions as carefully as possible in order for you to be chosen as an official arch tarot operator.

Your center piece is to be known as the tile. Your three sets of six tarot cards around the tile are to be known as the tile surround. One piece of the tile surround is to be known as a tile surround point. Your symbol placed onto the tile is to be known as the tile common. The pathway between your tile and your star is to be known as the tile light. When you are chosen by the arch to officially do arch tarot operations, you will be known as an arch tarot operator. When your sight is chosen by the arch to officially do arch tarot operations, it will be known as an arch tarot point. The rightmost tile surround point is to be equated as the eastern tile surround point and is the beginning or first point of your calculation. The bottommost tile surround point is to be equated as the southern tile surround point and is the middle or second point of your calculation. The leftmost tile surround point is to be equated as the western tile surround point and is the last or third point of your calculation. The topmost tile surround point is to be equated as the northern tile surround point and is the finish or equator of your tile surround, but it must be left blank by you, because the star finishes your tile surround equation for you. **refer to illustration 13**

Your tile needs to be completely square and the sides no larger in length than the height of three of your tarot cards with some extra space added between each card. Your tile can be made of anything that is of the right size and shape including: wood, plastic, stone, cloth, paper, or a drawing on a surface. It is always best to use the same tile, because the tarot spirits may become confused if they are presented with an unfamiliar tile. If your tile ever becomes damaged, you should replace it soon, because a damaged tile could lead to damaged life calculation results. **refer to illustration 14**

The type of tarot deck that you use is completely your choice. One separate tarot deck per tile surround point should be used just for that tile surround point, but it should never be moved to another tile surround point, because if another deck is used, the tarot spirits may become confused. If any of your tarot decks ever become damaged, you should replace them soon, because a damaged tarot deck could lead to damaged life calculation results.

Your tile common can be anything that is solid and anything that has good shape. The overall size of your tile common should not be any larger than the size of your tile. Your tile common should never appear dangerous or ever represent anything that is dangerous. Your tile common should always closely relate to the subject of your tile surround, because the tarot spirits may become confused if your tile common seems odd or unfamiliar. If your tile common ever becomes damaged, you should replace it soon, because a damaged tile common could lead to damaged life calculation results. **refer to illustration 15**

Your tile light is a communications transmission pathway for your life calculations between your tile and your star. The tarot spirits form the pathway for the tile light after your location has been accepted as an arch tarot point. The tile light will always be with your tile until you replace your tile or you move your tile to a different location.

The tarot spirits are provided to every single planet that has its own star by the arch. The tarot spirits are responsible for accepting you and your items and activating your location as an arch tarot point. The tarot spirits can never be seen by you, but if you are accepted by the arch as an arch tarot operator, the tarot spirits will be with you wherever you go. The tarot spirits that are associated with you are not your choice, but the choice of the arch, and only the arch can change them.

Every minute of every day, your star sends life calculations to the arch during its ready read state, and at any time throughout any day, you may commune with a king's chamber, queen's chamber, or assistant's chamber in your star using your tile surround. The crown's chamber must never be communed with by you, rather only by the kings' chambers, the queens' chambers, and the assistants' chambers. The chamber that you are communing with is not your choice, but the choice of the arch, and your position of chambers can never be changed unless the arch increases or decreases your position of chambers. **refer to illustration 13**

Each tile surround point consists of one tarot card, the capitol or the king's card, being closest to the tile, then two tarot cards, the column or the queen's cards, being below the first card, and then three tarot cards, the base or the assistant's cards, being below the second two. The capitol is always the lead or the transmitter of the tile surround point, the column is always the builder or the calculator of the tile surround point, and the base is always the provider or the informer of the tile surround point. After you choose your tarot cards for a tile surround point, the tarot spirits completely handle the informing, calculating, and transmitting for that tile surround point. **refer to illustration 13**

Any tarot card from the major arcana or minor arcana may be chosen by you using your own method for any tile surround point. You must always lay your tile surround point tarot cards from top to bottom and left to right starting with the eastern tile surround point and ending with the western tile surround point. When you are finished with your tile surround points, you then place your tile common onto your tile, and your tile light transmits your life calculations to your star, which sends your life calculations to its pyramil. **refer to illustration 16**

Illustration 13

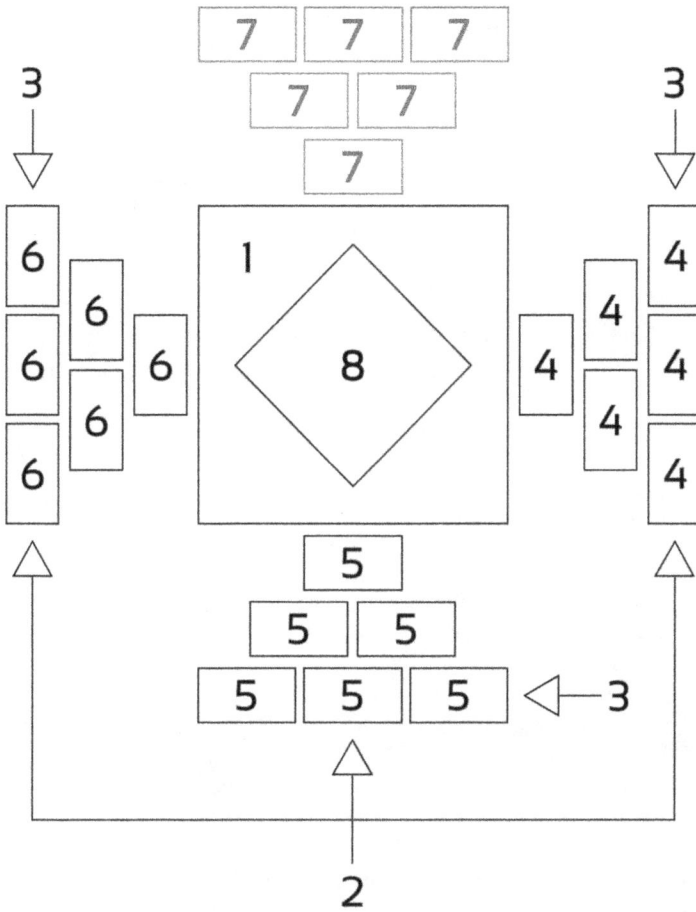

1: tile
2: tile surround
3: tile surround point
4: eastern tile surround point
5: southern tile surround point
6: western tile surround point
7: northern tile surround point
8: tile common

Illustration 14

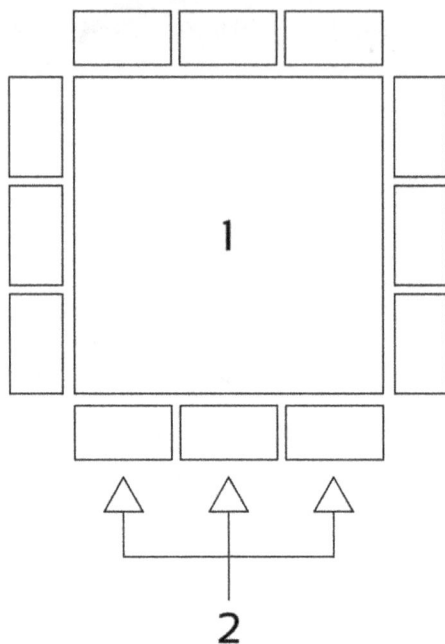

1: tile
2: three tarot cards with extra spaces

Illustration 15

1

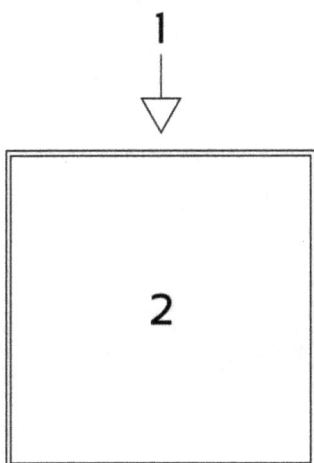

2

1: tile
2: maximum tile common size

Illustration 16

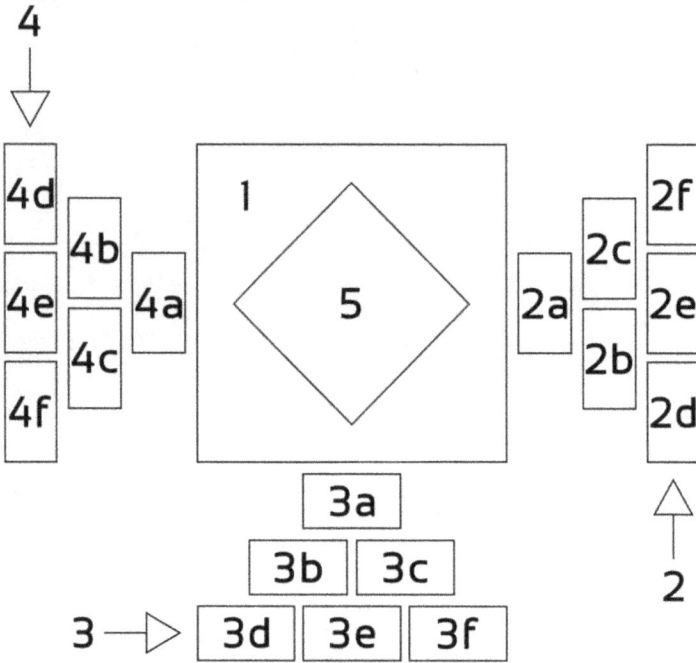

1: tile
2: eastern tile surround point
2a - 2f: eastern tile surround point tarot card pattern
3: southern tile surround point
3a - 3f: southern tile surround point tarot card pattern
4: western tile surround point
4a - 4f: western tile surround point tarot card pattern
2a: capitol
3a: capitol
4a: capitol
2b - 2c: column
3b - 3c: column
4b - 4c: column
2d - 2f: base
3d - 3f: base
4d - 4f: base
5: tile common

Poems, Writings, and Sayings

Of these poems, writings, and sayings of my own creation, I give to you for your benefit. I believe that when you remember them, read them, and speak them that many of the ancient spirits of your galaxy will find you, and if you prove yourself worthy, they will guide you throughout all of your tarot endeavours. If these poems, writings, and sayings never leave you, their spiritual benefit will be with you always.

Twelve Fantasy Poems to be Remembered

Long ago three elves did wait,
and wait a great time they did.
Until a chance to have a dance,
and at the crystal river they hid.

In the tower it must be,
a total of three rings it should send,
but if the tower is to fall,
unto a total of one it should not bend.

If the war den,
claws the tree,
a beacon's call,
there shall be.

So many rocks to be upon the shore,
so many say seven should be,
but if they ask for just one more,
fewer can say if any will see.

If an early death,
ever comes to me.
Then raised on rock,
my new son shall be.

Of a pilot be within the form,
but if the pilot be without the form,
a day becomes night within the form,
until the pilot without the form becomes reborn.

A wish upon a star may seem to be a baby's rhyme,
and playing again under the sun mere child's fun,
but when he came out the seventh and last time,
he knew then from early on that the saga had begun.

Millions survived to breathe life under the sun,
and the count of castles was the most large,
but the war of old could not be won,
until upon that gate they made their final charge.

Upon the path I learned to walk,
but not so tall until my grandmother spoke.
I never understood why my father loved to stalk,
until that new land I then proudly broke.

His powers were weak,
and considered ungreat.
Until the day he lifted,
that thirty ton weight.

For so many things a warrior can be without,
a special thing must be had to fight the hoard.
A fearful her did exist for many times,
until the day she carried that lightning sword.

A poem of old was needed for a spell,
but it was never found in any book.
Then thinking back she remembered the verse,
then into the mirror she did look.

Twelve Fantasy Writings to be Read

It is best to seek the safest road when many paths have become hazardous.

The safest way to the tower of light is with a kind heart and a loving mind.

If a task is so large that it cannot be completed, is it not best to seek assistance?

A wise secret is best kept covered with mysteries until it is time to use the secret's wisdom.

That which has less motion can be seen much easier, rather than that which has greater motion.

If any situation becomes too stressful, is it not best to seek a less stressful situation?

A thing is never worth doing unless the outcome can make the doer feel good.

It is best to seek the company of light and knowledge, rather than seeking the company of darkness and emptiness.

If one were to turn away before an answer is given, how would one ever discover the answer?

If too many items have become tainted, should they not be replaced with less tainted items?

Is it not best to do good things that are helpful, rather than doing bad things that are harmful?

A person is always best in no company, rather than in bad company.

Twelve Fantasy Sayings to be Spoken

Today we learn, today we write, today we speak.

I never had seen a true river dance, until the day that I saw the dance of the ferries.

It seemed so dark for so many times, until I discovered the painter of light.

A mystery is never discovered by an untrained mind.

A higher mind is never achieved by doing the things of a thief.

It is best to never yell or curse at any angry spirit.

Ancient paths are best travelled under a bright moon.

A beautiful thing was never created from anger or rage.

A good choice can never be made with a confused mind.

If I could have thought about it for some more time, I may have made a better decision.

A delicate thing cannot be kept safe in a place of rough handling.

In the still of the night is when the spirits may be heard.

Glossary

AmenDean: The arch during its life calculations transmission phase.

Arch: The device that communicates life calculations to all parts of a galaxy.

Arch Tarot Operator: A person chosen by the arch to officially do arch tarot operations.

Arch Tarot Point: A sight chosen by the arch to officially do arch tarot operations.

Area: A large particle expanse in the universe used to create things.

Arean: A great being of extreme particle wealth that was responsible for making many galaxies.

Arial: The largest device of the arch that is housed in a large sphere, which is in the center of a galaxy.

Assistant: A group of eight fourth commanders on an eye in an arial, spiral, pyramil, or star.

Assistant's Chamber: One of eight structures on an eye in an arial, spiral, pyramil, or star where the assistant's commands are housed.

Base: Three tarot cards that are the provider or the informer of a tile surround point.

Beacon: The life calculations that are sent by amendean.

Capitol: One tarot card that is the lead or the transmitter of a tile surround point.

Center: The central core in an arial, spiral, pyramil, or star.

Center House: The center part in a chamber on an eye in an arial, spiral, pyramil, or star.

Chamber: A structure on an eye in an arial, spiral, pyramil, or star where a command is housed.

Column: Two tarot cards that are the builder or the calculator of a tile surround point.

Commune: To speak to and to hear from another entity.

Compass Rose: A symbol that represents the sixteen main points of navigation.

Crown: The first commander on an eye in an arial, spiral, pyramil, or star.

Crown's Chamber: The structure on an eye in an arial, spiral, pyramil, or star where the crown's command is housed.

Eye: The platform attached to a tower in an arial, spiral, pyramil, or star that the crown's chamber, kings' chambers, queens' chambers, and assistants' chambers are attached to.

First Ring: The first circle of power formed when four kings become aligned on an eye in an arial, spiral, pyramil, or star.

King: A group of four second commanders on an eye in an arial, spiral, pyramil, or star.

King's Chamber: One of four structures on an eye in an arial, spiral, pyramil, or star where the king's commands are housed.

Galactic Area: An outer region of a space that contains an arch, planetary bodies, and particle flows.

Galactic Center: The center region of a space that contains an arch, planetary bodies, and particle flows.

Galactic Solar: A section of a portion of an outer region of a space that contains an arch, planetary bodies, and particle flows.

Galactic System: A portion of an outer region of a space that contains an arch, planetary bodies, and particle flows.

Galaxy: A space that contains an arch, planetary bodies, and particle flows.

Life Calculations: Information for particles and all living things that control many aspects of the natural world.

Lightcrown: A communications device on every chamber on an eye in an arial, spiral, pyramil, or star.

Lighthouse: A communications device on every room in every chamber on an eye in an arial, spiral, pyramil, or star.

Major Arcana: One suit of twenty-two tarot cards for the crown.

Minor Arcana: Four suits of fourteen tarot cards for four kings, their courts, and their associated assistants.

Pyramil: The third largest device of the arch that is housed in a large sphere, which is in the center of all galactic systems.

Queen: A group of four third commanders on an eye in an arial, spiral, pyramil, or star.
Queen's Chamber: One of four structures on an eye in an arial, spiral, pyramil, or star where the queen's commands are housed.

RayBeam: The small devices that communicate life calculations to all particles and living things with a powerful effect and influence.

Read State: The state of an eye in an arial, spiral, pyramil, or star in its unlocked position when it is first activated to be used.
Ready Read State: The state of an eye in an arial, spiral, pyramil, or star when it is reading life calculations after its first use.
Rest State: The state of an eye in an arial, spiral, pyramil, or star in its locked position before it is used.
Ring: A circle of power formed when three or more entities unite.
Room: The outer parts in a chamber on an eye in an arial, spiral, pyramil, or star where a sub-command is housed.

Second Ring: The second circle of power formed when four queens become aligned on an eye in an arial, spiral, pyramil, or star.
Send Sat State: The state of an eye in an arial, spiral, pyramil, or star when the assistants' chambers are aligned, the third ring is formed, amendean is aligned, and the beacon is sent.
Send Set State: The state of an eye in an arial, spiral, pyramil, or star when the queens' chambers are aligned, and the second ring is formed.

Send Sit State: The state of an eye in an arial, spiral, pyramil, or star when the kings' chambers are aligned, and the first ring is formed.

Send Sot State: The state of an eye in an arial, spiral, pyramil, or star when the crown's chamber is aligned.

Send Sut State: The state of an eye in an arial, spiral, pyramil, or star when the beacon is ready, amendean is activated, and the chambers expand.

Sent Sat State: The state of an eye in an arial, spiral, pyramil, or star when the assistants' chambers are dealigned, the third ring is deactivated, and amendean begins dealignment.

Sent Set State: The state of an eye in an arial, spiral, pyramil, or star when the queens' chambers are dealigned, and the second ring is deactivated.

Sent Sit State: The state of an eye in an arial, spiral, pyramil, or star when the kings' chambers are dealigned, and the first ring is deactivated.

Sent Sot State: The state of an eye in an arial, spiral, pyramil, or star when the crown's chamber is dealigned.

Sent Sut State: The state of an eye in an arial, spiral, pyramil, or star when the chambers contract into their ready read states, and amendean is completely dealigned.

Space: A large empty expanse in the universe after particles have been collected.

Spiral: The second largest device of the arch that is housed in a large sphere, which is in the center of all galactic areas.

Spirit: An invisible entity from the supernatural world capable of physically interacting with the natural world.

Star: The fourth largest device of the arch that is housed in a large sphere, which is in the center of all galactic solars.

Tarot: A carding system that bridges the gap between the natural world and the supernatural world.

Tarot Spirit: An invisible entity appointed by the arch to assist the natural world with tarot.

Third Ring: The third circle of power formed when eight assistant's become aligned on an eye in an arial, spiral, pyramil, or star.

Three Thousand Galaxies: An agreement between twelve areans to work together to create a peaceful place for people to live in happy ways.

Tile: The square center piece of an arch tarot point.

Tile Common: The symbol placed onto the square center piece of an arch tarot point.

Tile Light: The communications transmission pathway for life calculations between the square center piece of an arch tarot point and the closest star.

Tile Surround: Three sets of six tarot cards around the square center piece of an arch tarot point.

Tile surround point: One of the three sets of six tarot cards around the square center piece of an arch tarot point.

Tower: The rod attached between a center and an eye in an arial, spiral, pyramil, or star.

Even though I could have explained many things within this book in greater detail, I felt that you would not have achieved a true gift of power unless you learned and experienced some unwritten things for yourself.

After reading this book, I hope that the rest of your path to and through 'Three Rings Tarot' will be an enlightening and powerful experience for you.

I also hope that through great knowledge and wisdom you will use your three tile surround points to guide them all.

Always Remembered
The Core is always
the Lord of the Tower.

Always Read
The Tower is always
the Lord of the Crown.

Always Spoken
The Crown is always
the Lord of the Rings.

www.ingramcontent.com/pod-product-compliance
Lightning Source LLC
LaVergne TN
LVHW091210080426
835509LV00006B/929